MARINE HERITAGE GUIDE

The Sea Kingdom
ISLE OF MULL

Written by Rosalind Jones

Edited by Edward C.M. Parsons

Published by the Hebridean Whale and Dolphin Trust
June 2002

Printed by The Print Shop, Oban

This project is kindly funded by the following organisations

Contents

	PAGE
Who are the Hebridean Whale and Dolphin Trust?	3
Harbour Porpoises.	4
The walk from Tobermory to Bloody Bay.	5
Tobermory – founded on fish.	6
Fishing news from last century. Mull fishing today. Fish farming in Mull.	7
Wildlife in Mull.	8, 9
Otters take to the water. – A day in the life of an otter family.	10, 11
The Isle of Staffa.	12, 13
Mull Marine Heritage map.	14, 15
The Treshnish Isles.	16, 17
The quest of the sea eagle. – A day in the life of a young sea eagle.	18, 19
The turn of the tide. – A day in the life of a shore crab.	20, 21
The walk to Carsaig Arches.	22, 23
Shipwrecks around Mull.	24, 25, 26
Sea tales, folklore and legends of Mull.	27, 28

Credits

HWDT is very grateful to the following people for kindly donating the use of their pictures to the trust. Sarah Barry, Richard Evans, The Mitchell Library - Glasgow City Library, Clare Hoare, IFAW, Chris Jones, Nick Jones, Rosalind Jones, Phil Johnson, Andrew Livingstone, National Maritime Museum, Ben Osborne, Ocean Charters, Chris Parsons, Sea Life Surveys, Robert Snell, Alan Spellman, Jerry Sutton, Argyll & the Isles, Loch Lomond, Trossachs & Stirling Tourist Board.

HWDT and the author are very grateful to Susan MacKinnon of The Print Shop, Oban for her creative input into the design and layout of this publication, and Julie Paton, Clare Hoare and Cheryl Jones for their help with proof-reading this book.

Who are The Hebridean Whale and Dolphin Trust?

RESEARCH • EDUCATION • CONSERVATION

Established in 1994, the Hebridean Whale and Dolphin Trust (HWDT) is a registered Scottish charity dedicated to the conservation of whales, dolphins, porpoises (known collectively as cetaceans), and the marine environment. Through research, education and working with Hebridean communities, HWDT raises public awareness, promotes sustainable development and increases our understanding of the incredible marine diversity of the West Coast of Scotland

- Education Outreach and Monitoring Vessel

Purchased in 2002, the 65ft motor-sailing yacht 'Silurian' delivers an Outreach Education programme of school visits, public talks and events to islands and remote communities throughout the Argyll area. Travelling throughout the region, the Marine Ranger, Skipper and crew also monitor and report on marine mammals.

- Marine Interpretation and Education

The award-winning Marine Discovery Centre in Tobermory provides a range of exhibits and information on marine mammals for locals and visitors alike. HWDT also delivers a programme of talks and events, producing educational materials specific to our area.

- Community Sightings Project

HWDT encourages marine users, committed enthusiasts and visitors alike, to report sightings of marine mammals throughout Argyll and West Scotland. By doing so, they are contributing to our knowledge and understanding of cetacean behaviour and distribution throughout the region. This information is distributed at a national and international level.

- Bottlenose Dolphin Photo-Identification Project

West Scotland is the home to populations of dolphins about which little is known. Through this project we are identifying individual dolphins and learning more about the behaviour and distribution of this species.

- Working with Hebridean Communities

HWDT offers workshops and impartial advice to community groups throughout West Scotland, contributing to a wider understanding of the threats the marine environment faces.

- Conducting Research

Working with universities throughout the UK, and with local boat operators around the West Coast, HWDT has undertaken a variety of research projects. Recent projects include:

Minke Whale Photo-Identification - Working in conjunction with Sea Life Surveys, 76 individual whales have been identified in local waters.

Eco-tourism surveys throughout the West Coast of Scotland, determining the economic and social benefits of sustainable marine tourism development.

Land-based cetacean observation projects from the Ardnamurchan Lighthouse looking at minke whale habitat use and behaviour, as well as monitoring seasonal changes in cetacean abundance around the Ardnamurchan peninsula and the Small Isles.

- What Can You Do?

Marine conservation can be very land based and you don't need to be a marine biologist!

Use less and dispose of waste and rubbish carefully.

Lobby your MP over marine and whaling issues.

See whales in the wild! Boycott seeing whales and dolphins in captivity.

Support HWDT by:
Sponsoring a whale or dolphin
Naming a whale
Becoming a member
Becoming a Regional Co-ordinator

**Hebridean Whale and Dolphin Trust,
28 Main Street, Tobermory,
Isle of Mull PA75 6NU**

Tel: 01688 302620   Fax: 01688 302728
Registered Scottish Charity No. SCO22403
Company No. SC172338
To find out more about us, visit our website at

www.hwdt.org

Harbour Porpoises - *Phocoena phocoena*

FACT FILE

Harbour porpoises grow between 1.4 and 1.9m and have a short lifespan of about 9 years. The size of a new-born is between 67 - 88cm. Their numbers are declining due to a combination of 'bycatch' (accidental entanglement in fishing nets), prey depletion (decline of fish stocks due to commercial over fishing), noise pollution (cetaceans 'echolocate' by sounds which they produce and now man-made sounds in the sea are a hindrance) and habitat destruction. Echolocation isn't actually causing their decline but is another problem that they have to contend with. The main cause of decline is bycatch and pollution, but habitat destruction, noise and prey depletion place even more stress on these animals. They are handicapped in maintaining their population numbers by their short lifespan, - that they become sexually mature at a relatively late age, and only one calf is born from each pregnancy.

You can recognise harbour porpoises by their small rotund size, dark upper body colour and small round head with no beak. The smallest cetacean in UK waters, they surface quickly, showing only the small triangular dorsal fin. The harbour porpoise does not often exhibit the aerial leaps associated with some dolphin species but if they do emerge then their white lower body and pale sides can be observed.

These small cetaceans are usually sighted alone or in small groups of up to 10 individuals. Known as a peileag or muc in Gaelic the harbour porpoise is a resident species throughout the year in the Hebrides. They feed on small fish such as herring and whiting, but they also take a variety of other fish such as mackerel, cod and hake. When sprats and sand eels are plentiful they can be found feeding in the company of minke whales.

The Panorama from Bloody Bay to Calve Island

Bloody Bay — Ardnamurchan Point — Beinn nan Codhan — Beinn na Seilg — Kilchoan — ARDNAMURCHAN — Ben Hiant

The walk from Tobermory to Bloody Bay

Your chance to see Harbour Porpoises

A bay that once 'ran red' in one of the bloodiest naval battles ever fought in Hebridean waters is now a good place, with luck, to see harbour porpoises and it's only a one-hour, relatively easy return walk from Tobermory.

Starting at the Lifeboat shed at the end of Tobermory's main street a path leads up through the trees and levels off around the steep cliffs. In spring and summer you can smell the wild garlic that grows on the banks as you walk through a fringe of deciduous woodland with views down to the bay.

The cliff path is narrow, drops away on the seaward side, and is muddy with recent landslips, so stout shoes are necessary.

Views of the northern end of the Sound of Mull can be seen through the trees and when the vista opens out where the cliffs are heather-clad the wide entrance to Loch Sunart and the view across to Kilchoan on Ardnamurchan can be enjoyed. Stop at the viewpoint to enjoy the panorama from Bloody Bay to Calve Island.

FACT FILE

Bloody Bay inherited its name from the battle that took place around 1480 between father and son. John MacDonald of Islay, Lord of the Isles, was met in sea battle by his son Angus Og. 'Old' John was supported by Hector MacLean of Duart and his clan, whilst Angus was supported by Allan MacRuaraidh chief of Clan Ranald with his clansmen. In the sea battle in which the MacLeans of Mull, together with other clans fought for the Lord of the Isles, hundreds of galleys in the two rival fleets fought in close combat. The battle was so fierce that the bay ran red with blood and about 50 MacLeans were driven ashore where they hid in a cave under the cliffs. Here the fugitives were discovered by Angus's men, smoked out and killed. The cave is known as 'The Cave of the Heads' and last century, skulls and remains of human bones were found there.

MORVERN

Loch Sunart   Auliston Point   Drimnin House   Calve Island

Tobermory – founded on fish

The Burgh of Tobermory, the 'capital of Mull', was established in 1788. A small self-supporting settlement had existed there for centuries but in 1786 'The British Society for Extending the Fisheries and Improving the Sea Coast of the Kingdom', founded by the Duke of Argyll and the Earl of Breadalbane, decided that the sheltered harbour was ripe for development. In June 1787, directors of the Society sailed into the estuary of the River Aros, landing near the old castle. Once the home of the Lord of Isles and centre of Mull commerce, the importance of Aros was about to be usurped, for the party headed north to assess the possibilities of creating a purpose-built fishing station at the Well of Mary - Tobermory.

John, the 5th Duke of Argyll, generously entertained the party to a good dinner as he enthusiastically promoted the positive assets of Tobermory for the fisheries project. The weather was fair, the directors well fed, the bay and anchorage without equal, the fishing - untested. The decision was nevertheless made very quickly that Tobermory should become a model fishing station along with two others. (Ullapool, and Lochbay on Skye.) In March 1788, the Society feued the land from the Duke, and building began.

The Custom House was a key building for the fishing station as salt was essential for preserving the herrings they hoped to catch, and salt, until 1825, was taxed. Lodgings for Society employees, a storehouse, an inn, and finally a quay were the first buildings of the planned new town. Hoping to attract settlers from the island population, plots of land were laid out and feued, and the town planned on a grid pattern of spacious proportions.

In their decision-making, the British Fisheries Society as it came to be called, had not taken into account the difficulties in turning traditional farmers into fishermen, or the poverty of the people they hoped to interest in new homes, nor the distance from the herring grounds. This lack of forward planning could have spelt disaster for Tobermory; fishing did not take off as planned and the new town 'bubble' might have burst had not the 'Kelp Boom' happened. Alkaline ash from seaweed was used during the Napoleonic Wars in the manufacture of soap and glass. Planned by the Society for fishing, Tobermory pier was actually built in 1812-1814 by the Commissioners for Highland Roads and Bridges, following the kelp boom. The ensuing hard times in the 1820s when the kelp market collapsed at the end of the wars, lasted several decades, until Scotland became famed as a romantic location and visitors as notable as Mendelssohn and Queen Victoria sang the praises of Mull for tourists. They set the trend for future tourism that is the lifeblood of Tobermory today.

Fish caught in Mull's waters

Lesser Spotted Dogfish
Greater Spotted Dogfish
Porbeagle Shark
Spotted Ray
Cuckoo Ray
Blonde Ray
Thornback Ray
Common Skate
Conger Eel
Herring
Cod
Haddock
Poor Cod

Saithe/Coalfish
Whiting
Ling
Angler Fish
Red Gurnard
Grey Gurnard
Mackerel
Red Band Fish
Cuckoo Wrasse
Baillons Wrasse
Sand Eel
Turbot
Plaice
Dab
Halibut

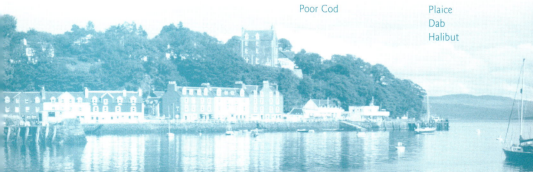

News cuttings from The Oban Times about fishing a century ago

On April 20th 1889 the following upbeat report was published.

'During the past few weeks a small fleet of seven fishing boats belonging to various ports in Aberdeenshire, has made Tobermory its headquarters. The fishing, both outside Coll and in local waters has been most successful. Almost every other morning 'The Pioneer' has had its consignments of from forty to seventy barrels for the English markets. Not far short of 400 barrels have already been dispatched. In addition tons of cod and ling have been retained already for curing. Curing establishments have been set up on Calve Island. The advantage of a regular morning steamer is a great one, and the proximity of fishing grounds.'

Although an honest account of 'good times for Tobermory fishing' it belied the overall situation of the ailing fishing trade. A long report from December 6th 1890 spoke of 'the destruction of our fisheries'.

It stated that less people were employed, there were fewer boats, and that the depression felt in the east coast fishing trade was just as keenly felt amongst the crofter-fishermen in the west who depended so largely upon fishing for their livelihood. This was followed on December 13th by an article about the Fishery Board of Scotland whose published statistics showed a worrying decline. Tobermory with its daily steamer connection to Oban and other west coast ports was, however, the best placed part of Mull for speedily processing its decreasing catch to markets. Fishermen in the Ross of Mull were not as well served and complained about the west of Mull mails on March 28th 1891.

'Last year the fisher folk of Loch Scridain side deplored the want of regular means of transit to the southern markets for their fish in a fresh condition. Had this communication existed, the harvest yield then by that far-reaching, fish teeming arm of the sea, would have been much greater than it was.'

The complaints about the mail service were well founded and improved communications were forthcoming as a report on September 19th showed:

'Good catches of herring of an inferior kind have been made in Loch Scridain in the end of the past week. The new mail service offers a ready transit for catches now.'

What Mull could not compete with though were the trawlers and 'the greedy meshes of the trawl net' and there was general gloom amongst the fishermen at the end of the 19th century about the marked decrease in the number of large cod being caught when this type of fishing began to expand.

Mull fishing today

The unproved stocks of fish that the British Fisheries Society hoped to exploit proved to be small and shoals of large cod, haddock and herring were soon fished out. Despite the loss of these Hebridean shoals there are still a great number and variety of fish for the angler to catch. Many fish caught off Mull in recent years have broken Scottish records so it's no wonder that keen sea anglers choose Mull for their fishing trips.

Fish farming in Mull

The British Fisheries Society could not have dreamt that one day Mull would become important for farming fish, notably salmon, but also trout. In those days Mull's rivers teemed with wild salmon and the freshwater lochs with trout. Today, although fish farming is an important producer and employs many islanders, many conservationists feel that it is an innovation that has spelt the demise of Mull's wild salmon. Natural wild salmon numbers caught have dropped dramatically year on year and this can be linked to fish farming as a cause. Farmed salmon are caged in huge numbers where parasite infestations build up, notably fish lice. Although farmed salmon are treated for these external parasites, their larvae escape the cages, develop into adults and infest the wild stock, weakening and killing them. Escaped farmed salmon which then interbreed with wild salmon produce young that no longer have pure, wild genes, and therefore instinct, are also thought to be a cause of decline. A problem is that the interbred salmon are unable to migrate to breeding grounds.

Studies show that fish farms also pollute the seabed under fish cages. Farmed fish are fed food pellets and some drop through the cage mesh onto the seabed. Excretory products from the salmon also drop through the mesh and unless there is a strong current to disperse this waste it builds up on the seabed, eventually killing organisms that cannot tolerate these waste products. Toxic chemicals used in fish farming practices are also released into the sea. Some fish farm companies are, however, working together with conservation bodies to reduce the environmental impact of fish farming.

Wildlife in Mull

Have you ever seen an otter eating its catch by a deserted loch as the sun slipped into the sea? Or mountain hares transfixed in your headlights in a lonely glen? Have you ever watched an eagle soar just overhead or seen a regal stag silhouetted against the skyline? If you haven't then this must be your first visit to Mull where scenes like these are commonplace yet never fail to excite lovers of wildlife.

Mull has a rich diversity of wildlife, more so than in any other island of the Hebrides, and with a little patience and insight it is not difficult to observe a large variety during even a short stay. Simply driving around Mull's coast-hugging roads is rewarding because herds of red deer grazing the mountainsides can often be seen. If you scan the sky over the mountains you can usually spot a golden eagle, or perhaps even the sea eagle with its greater wing span and white-feathered tail. Shaggy highland cattle may look wild but are domestic beasts more docile than their appearance suggests. Numerous species of sea birds abound and nobody can miss the lonely herons fishing the shorelines or the peeping flight of oystercatchers their red beaks contrasting against their black and white plumage. Stand still by a shore and if you see the bristly dog-like face of a seal emerge you are just as likely to be the object of observation by these inquisitive creatures. Although with luck you can get close, you have to stand very still and keep down wind if you see an otter. Short-sighted, these playful creatures are very shy and disappear if they detect you. Wild goats that roam Mulls' wildest coastlines will tolerate your presence if you watch them graze on their meal of sea weed from a respectful distance but move too close and the chief billy-goat will snort and the herd disdainfully leave you far below as they climb to their dizzy cliff-top retreats. Any chance sighting of these creatures is serendipitous but how do you go about really observing wildlife to best advantage on Mull?

If you have never watched wildlife before, or if your time is limited and you want to be rewarded with sightings then join one of the many wildlife trips, either day 'safaris' on land or sea trips many of which specialise in watching marine mammals, especially cetaceans. On organised trips you may be loaned binoculars but whether you go with a group or alone the following items are essential: binoculars or telescope, camera, notebook and pencil, handbook for identification, subdued or camouflaged clothing, good boots, and observant eyes! You don't need 20/20 vision simply the ability to use your eyes. Use them just like the animals use theirs – with an acute sense of awareness. Hear every sound, note the smallest of movements especially what you see in the corner of your eye, and respond to your own sixth-sense if you feel that you are being watched. Scan all around by moving your head left and right, up and down. You will cover more ground and by constantly scanning you will increase your chances of seeing the animals and their tracks and signs. Look again at anything that shows up pale or dark against the background because despite their camouflage, under the right conditions a great many animals can be visible over large distances. The rule is to note the unusual, how ever small the detail, and to remain constantly alert. Soon you will find that your new approach to wildlife watching has become second nature.

Otters are elusive creatures and will test your new wildlife watching skills. A good place to see otters is in a coastal location, often a promontory, near to woodland where mossy boulders can provide cover for their holt. Evening time is often the best time to watch otters as they prefer to emerge when man's daily activities have abaited. You can choose to sit very still and watch at one of the known places frequented by otters or stealthily cover large areas of the otter's loch-side home ground in the hope of a sighting. Despite their poor eyesight they can see you against the skyline, so crouch low and keep downwind because they have an excellent sense of smell. Avoid disturbing any other creatures that will give you away. If you do, pause and allow things to settle before moving again. With luck you will be rewarded with the sight of a flat whiskered head above the water followed by sinuous looping dives and perhaps the otter bringing ashore its catch and the noisy crunch of fish bones being masticated. Or it may float with the seaweed where it is so well camouflaged that you can only be sure of seeing it clearly when it moves.

Patience, keen observation, and even a good sense of smell are needed when watching on a sea trip. Mull's western seas are the place to see minke whales, harbour porpoises, Risso's, bottlenose, and common dolphins, and basking sharks. Initially every choppy wave looks like the fin of a cetacean or shark and it can feel as though you are looking for a needle in a haystack, but patience is generally rewarded. At about 10m long minke whales cannot remain invisible if they are in the vicinity. Often seen as they roll slowly out of the water they can be identified by the small, curved dorsal fin situated two-thirds back.

They have the habit of lunging with a resounding splash when feeding; their blow is barely visible but is accompanied by the smell of rotten cabbage. Watch through binoculars and be quick if you want to photograph them because their time at the surface is generally short before they disappear on dives that can last 20 minutes or more. Risso's dolphins, seen around Mull in summer months but resident in the Outer Hebrides reach lengths of 2.6 – 3.8m and are recognised by their blunt head, grey body and tall dorsal fin. Bottlenose dolphins are up to 3.9m long with distinct pointed noses and can be seen all year round almost hugging the coast. Common dolphins are regular summer visitors in large groups. They are 1.7 – 2.4m long with a distinctive hour-glass pattern. Dolphins may treat you to their acrobatic aquatic displays, whilst basking sharks, 7m filter feeders, steadily trawl the surface with gaping mouths unconcerned by boats or whale-watchers!

Seals are best seen basking on their offshore islets. Both grey (or Atlantic seals) and common seals are found around Mull where they come ashore to give birth to their pups. Some seal colonies have little contact with man and show a great interest in visiting boats. Common seals in particular, with their dog-like heads and appealing eyes, like to give visitors the once over. Their seeming friendliness, and graceful underwater gyrations, can be so beguiling that many a visitor has had to resist the temptation to join them.

FACT FILE

To photograph wildlife and be rewarded with excellent shots requires time, patience, and in the case of nesting birds or really elusive creatures – a hide. You must realise that you will be an unsettling intrusion who could upset breeding birds or animals. Details of how to photograph a ground nesting bird, such as an oystercatcher: preparation must be made over several days, with each bout of ten minutes or less, and with the minimum of disturbance. Day 1. A heavy duty canvas hide with poles (either bought or made) and netting to incorporate local material. Heap these on the ground no nearer than 50 metres from the nest. Day 2. Move the pile 25 metres from the nest and add more local material. Day 3. Move pile to 10 metres from the nest and quickly erect hide (no higher than 1.3m), and weave in camouflage vegetation into the netting. Day 4. Move hide closer but no nearer than 4m. Pin a dummy lens (the bottom of a plastic bottle is ideal) to the front of the hide. Day 5. Arrive early, before dawn if possible, together with a companion. Remove dummy lens and replace with camera on a tripod. Friend leaves the hide, thereby deceiving the subject into thinking it is alone. As some birds are frightened by the camera shutter noise it is advisable to play a tape recording of the shutter sound. Even when played softly at first the bird may fly off and once it returns you must wait for at least 20 minutes so that the bird bonds with its eggs or chicks again before trying again. Increase the volume little by little and only when the sound is the same as the shutter volume, and the bird at ease, should you take the photograph. Remember to dismantle the hide afterwards and remove.

Otters take to the water

Dawn's rosy light lit the moss-covered boulders of the otter's holt. Snuggled inside beside her sleeping cubs the mother otter stirred. The nest space was confined, her cubs, a male and a female, had grown large and her sensitive nose prodded their thickly furred bodies before she wriggled to the entrance to assess the day. Short-sighted, peering towards the loch her nose told her more about the morning than her eyes.

It had rained heavily in the night breaking the spring drought, and the air was washed clean. Amongst other information her keen nose picked up the smell of her mate, the large dog otter who had fed her and her cubs for two months since their birth. She had not seen him for nearly a month since the cubs were weaned. Her cubs did not stir. Used to their mother's morning hunt for food, they had no inkling that today would be any different.

Gently nudged awake, they whimpered in high pitched voices anticipating breakfast. Surprised to discover there was none they scrambled questioningly after her, following suit as she slid down the wet path between small twisted oak, birch and rowan trees. Sliding was a game, and the mother otter knew that today's lessons should be disguised as games if she was to teach her cubs to swim. Scampering down the slope, her longer back legs curiously arching her body as she ran, she whistled shrilly and her cubs replied with high pitched piping sounds as half hidden in the tussock grass they followed. Pausing to let them catch up, she stood up on her hind legs and sniffed the air.

The cubs clambered on to a stump of bogwood where, during the night, their father had marked his territory. His spraint a black slimy twist, still shiny and fresh. His musk was familiar and they quickly lost interest preferring to slip between concealing tussocks and slide over the grassy edge into the streambed where they sometimes played. Just a trickle during the drought the stream was swollen by the night's rain and the cubs hastily scrambled out. Disconcerted they chattered querulously as they briskly shook themselves, the dark guard hair of their pelts clumping into furry spikes. The mother otter nuzzled them encouragingly and led them off again, following the stream towards the loch. Their familiar route suited her purpose very well.

Naturally water-shy, the young otters quickly found it did them no harm and they followed to where a shallow pool had filled. Here their mother turned over playfully revealing her creamy underside. Rolling acrobatically in the water she encouraged them to join her and soon all three were cavorting, wrestling, and biting each other's tail tips as they chased back and forth across the pool. The sun was higher when she led them on again, splashing through the riffles but swimming alone in the pools. Insecure, her cubs chattered as they watched. Eventually she led them under the arch of a road bridge. On the further side was a deep pool and into this she dived, disappearing without a ripple. Her cubs peered sceptically over the edge. Beneath the surface they watched her circle gracefully, a path of bubbles rising from the fur of her supple body and long tail. With valves and hairs closing her nostrils and small ears but eyes wide open, she scouted for fish, pushing her muzzle into every cranny but nothing edible touched her sensitive whiskers.

Submerged for two minutes in the silky water she surfaced to find her cubs distressed. They piped shrilly as she emerged sleek and wet. Before they knew what was happening she had butted them in! Buoyant with their baby under-fur they did not sink but paddled frantically on the surface, the claws on their webbed feet clutching at the pool side to escape. Undignified they scrambled out hastily and shook themselves, their thick under-fur still dry. Diving in again their mother surfaced immediately calling them to join her as she swam across the pool, but they ran over the dry rocks instead, leaving behind small webbed footprints.

The stream braided downstream, entering the loch as a pebbly delta. This place was often a good place to catch fish on an incoming tide but the tide was still low and hunger gnawed, so the mother otter led her cubs by the rocky shoreline where they investigated the salty seaweed and watched the black and white oystercatchers fly past. Waves rolled in unexpectedly making the cubs jump in surprise, but they became more confident when they reached a sandy bay full of cockleshells and seaweed covered rocks. The tide was out and they started to explore.

Pushing her whiskered head under festoons of slippery, knotted wrack seaweed the adult emerged with a shore crab in her mouth, legs arched and pincers open. Holding it delicately in her front paws her sharp canines crunched its carapace, and biting through its shell she tore pieces off for her cubs. Then she found another crab but did not kill it. She dropped it and nudged it with her nose. The crab remained still, then scuttled sideways. She pounced on it, retreated, leaving it unmolested until it moved again. Inquisitive, the cubs nosed it and she backed away leaving them to pounce on it, one of them experimentally biting it before dropping it again. The other cub took the injured prey and ate it. The crunching noises encouraged the other to search under the weed until it grabbed a crab by its legs and fed too.

Emboldened by their success the two cubs continued searching, finding the crabs as much a game as a means of satisfying hunger. The tide had turned and their mother, now in deep water by the rocks, had caught a large flatfish. Sharp canines gripping it firmly she emerged from the water as her cubs, still hungry, scampered to join her. Overhead a sea eagle, huge wings outspread as it circled loch and shore, silhouetted the afternoon sky. In the shelter of the rocks the adult otter tore off pieces to share with her cubs, their molars noisily grinding the fish bones to pulp before swallowing. Then, leaving the fish head behind but with a fleshy piece of tail she enticed her cubs into the water where she lay on her back firmly clutching her lure. As one cub clambered onto her belly to take the tail she pushed off with her back legs and drifted into deeper water where she submerged leaving her cub frantically paddling, its calls of distress echoed by its sibling crouching in a crevice on the shore. Emerging, the mother otter called shrilly and her cub swam easily towards her. Just at that moment a car stopped by the loch side and a couple with their dog got out and binoculars trained on the sky. Bounding down to the water where it smelt the otter cub in its hiding place the soft-mouthed dog picked it up triumphantly. Shrill noises from the cub and from the loch alerted the people.

'It's an otter! Drop it!!' they both shouted.

The dog dropped the cub in surprise and the young otter, unharmed but terrified, dashed to join its mother and sibling. Impelled by danger the cub overcame its fear, its webbed feet and long muscular tail finding their true element at last.

As the couple watched them through their binoculars they saw a large dog otter, diving and surfacing in sinuous loops, join them. Unobserved, except by the forlorn dog, the sea eagle swooped down and swiftly stole the fish head the otters had left behind.

The Isle of Staffa

Staffa is composed of the earliest of the outpourings of basalt lava, the Fingal's Cave Lava of the 'Staffa Suite'. This thick lava flow solidified into large hexagonal columns that characterise the isle. The lava is underlain by red ash that can be seen from Fingal's Cave and along most of the west coast. The lava divided into a lower zone of massive regular columns with sides varying in number between 8 and three though the average is six, a middle zone of narrow wavy columns, and a top zone that is mostly slag. Most people approach the cave along the causeway where the horizontal joints which cross-cut the columns into useful steps. At Fingal's Cave the two columnar zones are well exposed. In the columns here, calcite, which is secondary in formation, appears to 'cement' the columns together. It was for this reason that when first discovered it was assumed that Staffa was man-made (by a race of giants) because the stones were cemented together. The base of the lava, which is vesicular (bubbly) and brecciated (broken up) can be seen at Port an Fhasgaidh. The slaggy (rubbly top) zone can be seen for 300 yards south of the Goat cave.

Impressions of Staffa

SIR JOSEPH BANK'S VISIT TO STAFFA IN 1772

Sir Joseph Banks, (president of the Royal Society 1778-1819) was actually en-route to Iceland when a chance meeting with a resident of Morvern led to his visit to Staffa. He was so entranced with the isle, which he felt was superior to man's palaces and cathedrals, that he wrote

> "the mind can hardly form an idea more magnificent than such a place, supported on each side by ranges of columns and roofed over by the bottom of those which have broken off from it, between the angles of which a yellow stalagmite matter has exuded which serves to define the angles precisely and at the same time vest the columns with a great deal of elegance and to render them more agreeable. The whole is lighted from without so that the furthest extremity is very plainly seen from without."

He spent a night camping on the isle and even left his initials 'J.B.1772' at the farthest part of the cave.

SIR WALTER SCOTT'S POEM 'THE LORD OF THE ISLES' Includes this verse

"The shores of Mull on the Eastward lay
And Ulva dark and Colonsay
And all the group of islets gay
That guard famed Staffa round.
Then all unknown its columns rose
Where dark and undisturbed repose
The cormorants had found
And shy seal had quiet home
And weltered in that wondrous dome
Where as to shame the temples deck'd

By skill of early architect
Nature herself, it seemed would raise
A Minster to her maker's praise
Not for a meaner use ascend
Her columns, or her arches bend
Nor of a theme less solemn tells
That mighty surge that ebbs and swells
And still, between each awful pause,
From the high vault an echo draws."

FAUJAS DE ST FOND IN 1784

So impressed was Sir Joseph that he made the phenomenon known to the eminent French geologist Faujas de St Fond who undertook, in 1784, the then difficult journey from France to see the natural wonder. He was the first geologist to visit Staffa. Despite being horribly seasick Faujas de St Fond was amply rewarded by his discoveries on Staffa. He wrote

> "I ceased not to view, to review and to study this superb monument of nature, which in the regularity of its form bears a strong resemblance to a work of art…"

He took measurements whilst a companion, who tossed around in a skiff near the entrance to Fingal's Cave, made sketches. Faujas noted that the draughtsman used by Sir Joseph Banks to illustrate Fingal's cave had lazily relied on imagination when it came to drawing the chaotic rocky layer above the tall columns, drawing boulders instead of small irregular columns. This wasn't good enough for the critical eye of Faujas who correctly surmised that the hexagonal nature of the columns was due to a gradual cooling and shrinking of the lava.

SIR CHARLES LYELL 1817

Sir Charles Lyell was a founding father of British geology and he visited Staffa in 1817, the small boat he was in being sucked in and out of Fingal's Cave with the ebb and flow of the tide. He marvelled at the echo within the cave, and at skill of his boatmen who also took him into the Boat Cave about which he commented

> "The pillars are ranged in a fine swell on each side, instead of being straight in the manner of a wall."

FELIX MENDELSSOHN 1829

Felix Mendelssohn together with his friend Karl Klingermann visited Staffa in rough weather. The cave made an enormous impression on Felix and he was inspired to compose the beginning of his Hebridean Overture. The main theme came to him whilst he was in the Fingal's Cave and he was anxious to try out the tune as soon as he arrived back at his host's house but because it was Sunday, the piano was not to be played. Happily Felix managed to persuade his host to make an exception in his case – otherwise the evocative tune might have been lost forever!

QUEEN VICTORIA 1847

Queen Victoria visited Staffa whilst on a cruise around Scotland's West Coast with Prince Albert, their two eldest children, and her brother Charles. She wrote in her diary

> "At three we anchored close before Staffa and immediately got into the barge with Charles and the children and the rest of our people and rowed towards the Cave. As we rounded the point the wonderful basaltic formation came into sight. The appearance it presents is most extraordinary; and when we turned the corner to go into the renowned Fingal's Cave, the effect was splendid, like a great entrance into a vaulted hall: it looked almost awful as we entered and the barge heaved up and down."

She noted the unusual colours to be seen below water in the cave.

> "The rocks under water were all colours, pink, blue, green, which had the most wonderful effect."

A very popular monarch, the seamen raised three cheers to her because it was the "first time the British Standard with a Queen of Great Britain and her husband and children had entered Fingal's Cave."

FACT FILE

The best places to see Dolphins, Porpoises, Otters and Seals from land.

PORPOISES
Pennygown, Fishnish Ferry, Ardmore, Bloody Bay, Grass Point, Duart Castle, and the ferry to Mull around Lismore lighthouse.

OTTERS
Pennyghael, Carsaig, Loch na Keal.

SEALS
Salen, Loch na Keal and Treshnish Isles.

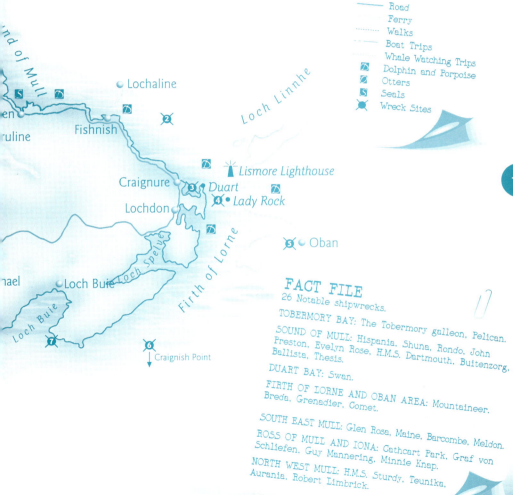

KEY

- Road
- Ferry
- Walks
- Boat Trips
- Whale Watching Trips
- Dolphin and Porpoise
- Otters
- **S** Seals
- Wreck Sites

FACT FILE
26 Notable shipwrecks.

TOBERMORY BAY: The Tobermory galleon, Pelican.

SOUND OF MULL: Hispania, Shuna, Rondo, John Preston, Evelyn Rose, H.M.S. Dartmouth, Buitenzorg, Ballista, Thesis.

DUART BAY: Swan.

FIRTH OF LORNE AND OBAN AREA: Mountaineer, Breda, Grenadier, Comet.

SOUTH EAST MULL: Glen Rosa, Maine, Barcombe, Meldon.

ROSS OF MULL AND IONA: Cathcart Park, Graf von Schliefen, Guy Mannering, Minnie Knap.

NORTH WEST MULL: H.M.S. Sturdy, Teunika, Aurania, Robert Limbrick.

The Treshnish Isles

The Treshnish Isles can be likened to emeralds strung in a SW-NE chain in Mull's western sea. Each uniquely shaped by pre-glacial marine erosion from a ridge of basalt lava flows, the six main islands can be characterised by words beginning with 'b'. Two miles from the mainland of Treshnish Point are the twin isles of Cairn na Burgh More and Cairn na Burgh Beg. These are the *barracks* with ruins of two small forts. Once a Viking outpost, English red coat soldiers were garrisoned here in 1745 during the search for Bonnie Prince Charlie. Larger Fladda lives up to its name and is as flat as a *billiard* table, whilst the largest isle, Lunga has a silhouette like a *battleship*. Bac Mor or 'Dutchman's Cap' has a profile more like a Mexican som*brero*. Finally, connected at low tide to Bac Mor by a causeway is Bac Beag, which with a highest point of 27m compared to Bac Mor's 86m is shaped more like a *biscuit*. There is, however, only one word beginning with 'b' that describes them all – *beautiful*!

The islands are owned by the Hebridean Trust, and are important for several reasons. They are a special protected area for seabirds and a special area for conservation to protect the seal colonies on the islands. No longer stocked with sheep the wild flowers are able to grow unimpeded by grazing and make a luxuriant show in spring and summer. The apparent fertility has much to do with the amount of guano, the natural fertiliser obligingly provided by the islands' sea birds. Cliffs and stacks are the nesting sites for thousands of guillemots, fulmars, razorbills, kittiwakes, black guillemots, and shags, whilst the islands' most popular attraction – puffins, nest in holes near the cliff edges.

In season, there are several boats that take visitors to the Treshnish Isles, landing - weather permitting - on Lunga for two hours' exploration. It's a trip that many regard as the highlight of their holiday. There is so much to discover and a large area to cover. Most sites of interest can be seen along the coastal route. Walk in an anti-clockwise direction from the path that leads from the boulder strewn landing beach. The first 'distraction' you encounter are the puffins that seem almost as interested in you as you are in them. Approach carefully on all fours because their fragile homes and chicks are just below the surface and can easily be squashed. Adults emerge from their burrows, line up along the cliff edge, turning their heads engagingly as they inspect you, before flying off to collect sandeels for their young. Many visitors don't stir themselves to look any further, so charming are the puffins and their seemingly comical behaviour, but these natural clowns are just one of the 52 different species listed for Lunga. Continue south along the cliff path to see the birds nesting on the magnificent sea stack. If you try to count those you can see you'll find it impossible and the noise they make can be deafening. Amongst the tumbled rocks at this location you can also see Shags nesting. They do not like inquisitive visitors and will tell you so – vociferously. You can climb to the cairn marking the 103m summit of Lunga and enjoy panoramic views over Mull and to the Isles of Coll and Tiree. But if you'd like to see more birds and the chance to see the seals, Common and Grey, basking on rocky islets then continue to walk around the hilly part towards the eastern side.

This will mean that you don't have time to see the flat part of Lunga and you'll be terribly torn between wanting to see what is to be discovered there and what lies waiting in the east. If time presses and you mustn't be late, return to your boat along the eastern path and see the more 'exclusive' nesting sites of Lunga's birds on ledges lining deep ravines. Fewer birds are to be seen here but individuals are easier to observe and study.

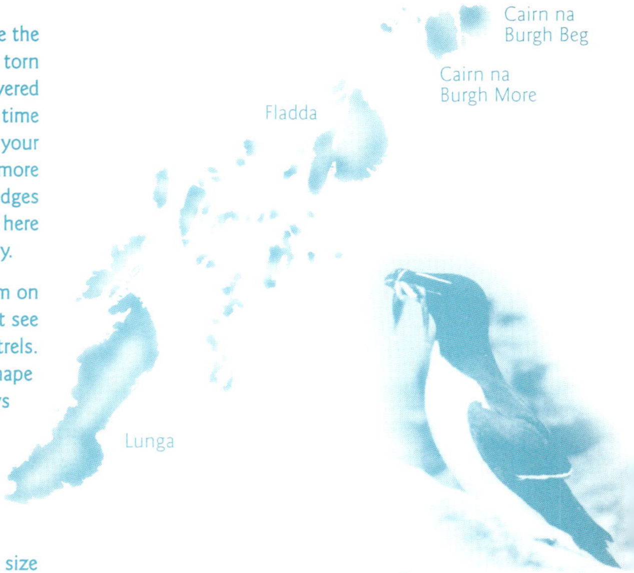

Unless you are very lucky and observe them on your sea trip to or from the islands, you won't see any of the island's 5,000 pairs of storm petrels. These tiny birds, that are only the size and shape of a house martin or swallow, breed in burrows in the ground taking it in turns to incubate their eggs. Change-over occurs at night, the male flying straight into the nest and the female flying straight out. Covering long distances on these foraging flights they feed on plankton and despite their small size survive long hours alone on the ocean. The few Manx shearwaters that breed on the island and share the same habits are just as elusive, as is the corncrake whose strident call can sometimes be heard – but is rarely seen.

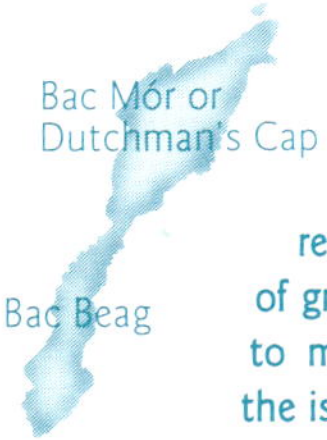

As you pass Fladda on your return journey look out for a flock of greylag geese that return annually to moult in protected isolation on the island.

Cairn na Burgh Beg

Cairn na Burgh More

Fladda

Lunga

Bac Mór or Dutchman's Cap

Bac Beag

FACT FILE

Puffins, members of the auk family. Puffins do not live all the year on the Treshnish Isles but return each spring. They excavate existing burrows in peaty turf on cliff edges where they nest, laying one dull white egg. They swim and dive expertly to catch fish, mostly sandeels. Puffins have a familiar brightly coloured bill that is used to attract a mate. It's razor sharp edge is good for gripping fish. The bright colours on the bill fade in winter. The least vocal of the auks they have a creaking, growling call heard in the breeding season only.

The quest of the sea eagle

The sea eagle watched a hooded crow picking the bones of a hare on a rocky knoll opposite his eyrie. The hare was the young eagle's last kill, discarded two days earlier. From his treetop in the lee of a vast ice plucked rock, the three-year old male watched the crow with predatory interest. The sun was still behind the mountains and he was hidden in shadow. Crows are wily and if this carrion-eater was to become his breakfast, the sea eagle knew he would have to surprise it, for the crow would fly as soon as it detected any sudden movement. Gripping the branch with sharp clawed, yellow feet he poised to launch himself. His hooked beak, turning yellow with increasing maturity, gaped slightly as his tongue licked the roof of his mouth. His keen eyes scrutinised his prey - he was hungry.

As soon as the sun's rays pierced the skyline, lighting the knoll, the sea eagle leapt. With the sun at his back he wouldn't be seen easily. But the beat of his huge wings alerted the crow. It dropped the carcass and flew away, cawing raucously. Slow in pursuit, the sea eagle gradually gained on the bird as it flew down into the glen where it often perched on the telephone cable opposite the bird table of a small cottage. Instead of this open position the cunning bird found safety between the ceramic insulators on the telegraph pole where it cawed stridently. A woman walking her dog in the fields looked up attracted by the sounds and saw the wide silhouette and unmistakeable white feathers developing in its once brown tail. Unconcerned by woman, or barking dog, the sea eagle circled, watching the crow. Finally, defeated by the crafty bird, the eagle emitted a high-pitched call before beating his two metre span wings to climb high over the hillside opposite towards the northern hills.

Undeterred by his failure, the sea eagle flew northwest, the boggy treads and rocky risers of the stepped tableland beneath him lit by rosy morning light. There were ground nesting birds to be found here, rabbits and hares. Sheep were grazing below him, nibbling grass washed by a night of rain after the long spring drought. Nimble lambs closely followed their shaggy mothers. Flying higher he scouted for any tell tale patch of white against the green. Stillborn lambs, though skinny, would make an adequate meal. All he found was the remains left by a golden eagle – pecked clean by crows. Cresting the hills, the sea around the island of Ulva looked like beaten metal so bright was the sun. Soaring on up-draughts over the heights he noted a straggle of people hurrying towards a motorboat at the jetty. Keeping to high ground the young sea eagle winged north intent upon patrolling the summits overlooking Loch Tuath.

Golden plovers nesting near the hilltops crouched protectively over their chicks as he flew overhead. In a rocky hollow he saw a solitary red deer with her newborn calf. The hind watched warily when he landed close by hoping for a meal of afterbirth, but she had already eaten it. Intimidated by the sea eagle the hind moved off, her calf staggering to its feet to follow on wobbly legs. He watched their retreat before excited calls commanded his attention, and looking skyward near the south end of Ulva he saw the cart wheeling aerial display of mature sea eagles' courting. He watched their figures colliding in mid-air, their talons gripping at each other. The female, lighter in colour, larger and heavier, seemed the dominant of the pair. Knowing better than to fly that way into possible conflict he preened his dark brown feathers until a solitary sea gull flew over the hilltop, and the young eagle took off to follow. Sea gulls made good meals. Realising it was being pursued the gull flew faster but the eagle was soon close enough to grab the bird.

Innately agile, the sea gull dropped away to the safety of the seashore far below. The sea eagle dived after it. Flying over a rocky headland he was within a talons grasp of catching it when three greater black-backed gulls pecking at something on the shore distracted him as they flew off in alarm. The smell of rotting flesh and the sight of a young porpoise washed up on the narrow, rocky beach offered an easier meal. Taking care to keep away from the tide that was advancing, he continued the scavenging work started by the black-backs. Tearing off flesh with his hooked beak he ate quickly for waves were lapping the carcass. Too soon the sea eagle was forced to fly away, before the tide left him no beach from which to take off.

With powerful, ponderous wing beats he flew high over Loch Tuath. Around the north of Ulva he saw the Staffa motorboat returning. In the bright sunshine the Treshnish Isles looked vivid green. Deciding not to fly out to Lunga, where sometimes he caught unwary puffins leaving their burrows, he rode the thermals rising above the warm black basalt rocks of the island. Circling higher and higher, his wings' horizontal and primary feathers spread wide, he surveyed the scene. Far below flashes of sunlight reflected from binoculars trained upon him from the motorboat as he soared, swooped, and rose, circling the heights. Crowding the open deck, trippers on the boat watched his majestic flight.

The trippers had driven away in their cars before the sea eagle winged homeward again. Following the coast this time he turned eastwards into Loch na Keal. He had almost reached the head of the loch when he saw, on rocks near a sandy bay, a family of otters. Otters meant the chance of another meal for they often caught more fish than they consumed and obligingly left uneaten remains where they came ashore. He could see an adult otter and two cubs and he watched from above as the adult and one cub swam away leaving the other by the rocks. He was about to land to chase the otter cub away when a car pulled up and two people got out. He saw them watching him so he circled, waiting. He witnessed the commotion as their dog caught the remaining cub, but he saw the dog drop it and the otter escape. Watching the otter family swim away he saw a larger otter join them. Noticing the people's attention drawn to the bay, their glasses trained on the sea, he swooped down and retrieved the remains of a flatfish. Only the dog saw him, and growled, its hackles bristling.

The sea eagle took off with powerful wing beats clutching a fish head. Flying over stunted woodlands and open grassland, then via the hilltops of the southern mountains he arrived back at his favourite eyrie. Soaring up and over the giant crag he hovered above the cliff edge, to land very gently, in his tree.

The turn of the tide

The shore crab edged out from the crevice where he had spent the night, protected from waves breaking on the rocky shore. Wind driving the waves during the night had dropped and the calm sea surface now reflected the pink glow of dawn. The moon had been full during the night and the tide had encroached higher up the shore, wetting tar-black lichens on the rocks. Now the tide was falling, exposing short rubbery fronds of green-brown channel wrack to become dehydrated, black and brittle if the day remained dry. Minute periwinkles, and larger ones with rough, grey pointed shells, were already tucked into tiny cracks, their door-like plates covering the opening of their shells shuttered tight to avoid desiccation. The shore crab did not care for these small snails or the green woodlouse-like ocean-slaters that roamed the splash zone, he never ventured up to the top of the shore for such poor pickings. Instead he roamed the middle and lower shore where, with his green shell the colour of the seaweed that clung thickly to the rocks, he was camouflaged and could survive more easily.

Close to the landward limits of his territory, the mature male crab scurried between fronds of spiral wrack twisting in the tide's ebb and flow. Limpets that lived here were gliding back home, rasping encrusting algae with file-like tongues from the smooth rock, as they journeyed back to the same oval depression they had left. Higher on the middle shore, some were already suckered down, their head, tentacles, and muscular foot hidden within their steep conical shell. Knowing he would be unsuccessful attacking those already fixed to the rock the crab waited amongst the weed to ambush any unwary creatures in the vicinity. His mouth-parts moved mechanically in hungry expectation.

He was too slow to catch a transparent shrimp whose long antennae had accidentally touched his own but a homeward-bound limpet, meandering around the holdfasts of spiral wrack, was a prize victim. The crab's sharp pincers shot outwards, missing the limpet's small head but nipping a tentacle. Instantly the shell clamped down and despite agitated attempts proved impossible for the shore crab to budge. Encrusting barnacles filtering food from the water nearby were alerted by the commotion and they immediately withdrew their tiny jointed legs and closed their shutter-like plates. Flicking his small five-jointed tail folded under its belly the crab backed away, disturbing plum-red beadlet anemones that quickly withdrew their tentacles safely inside their sac-like bodies. The hungry crab skittered to buoyant knotted-wrack whose egg-like bladders held the long leathery fronds erect. In deeper water now where the rocks gave way to sand, he was in a veritable forest of seaweed that swayed gently as the tide retreated.

Variedly coloured flat periwinkles, green, brown, yellow, and orange, grazed the knotted and bladder wrack that grew together in this region of the shore. The crab needed all the enhanced eyesight that his compound eyes offered to detect the snails because their rounded shells with flattened spires, coloured so much like the bladders of the seaweed, hid them very well. Expertly he climbed the knotted wrack, his four pairs of back legs resting delicately on swollen reproductive nodules ripening with eggs soon to be shed into the water. He waited immobile, concealed behind a festoon of polyzoa, tiny plant-like animals growing on the frond. The tide was steadily dropping when a large orange snail glided back down the lengthy frond whose tip was now prostrate on the surface.

Infinitely carefule, the crab manoeuvred his pincers into position to intercept the flat periwinkle, its vulnerable head-foot never leaving the crab's sharp sight. As it passed, the camouflaged crab's pincers flashed out, and the tentacles and siphoned head of the unwary snail were gripped fast. The soft flesh was quickly, and fastidiously devoured, by slicing movements of his armoured mouthparts. The shell was discarded and sank to join other empty shells on a patch of sand below. Unobserved by the crab, a tiny hermit crab living inside a smaller periwinkle shell dragged himself over to the new shell, inspecting it carefully before quickly transferring his soft body into this larger home. Shuffling back to the shelter of overhanging rock the hermit shut his 'front door' provided by his armoured pincers.

Scuttling down the weed the still hungry shore crab made its way between fronds of bladder-wrack and through serrated saw-wrack to a point where a raft of mussels clung by their tough threads to a rocky edge. Two dog whelks, siphons waving alongside their brown and white-banded spires, were moving away satiated. Telltale holes drilled neatly in some now empty mussel shells showed where the dog-whelks had dined. A common starfish was still eating, its suckered arms clamped on one of the blue-black molluscs, pulling the two shells apart so it could feed. The crab examined the mussel bed looking for any that might have been damaged the night before. Gaping slightly as their frilly-edged siphons filtered food particles suspended in the water, the mussel's valves shut abruptly as he tiptoed over them. But he was in luck. At the edge of the colony were two mussels with smashed shells, their flesh still inside. Pulling out pieces of creamy-coloured mussel he was feasting on one when a menacing shape loomed in front of him. It was a female shore crab. Larger, with a seven-jointed tail protecting a bag of tiny crab eggs stuck to her underside, and with bigger pincers raised aggressively,

the female moved towards the smaller male in a threatening manner. Instinctively he raised his own pincers but as the female advanced he backed away. Leaving the remaining mussel, the male dropped to the sand below and scuttled sideways to a rock draped completely in festoons of seaweed lowered by the receding tide. Thick-shelled edible winkles were still grazing as the crab tucked himself under a curtain of weed. Concealed he watched, as the marauding female, her stolen meal finished, selected the same rock for shelter as the tide reached the leathery straps of brown kelp and left the shore exposed to the warm sunshine of the day.

Protected from drying amongst the moist covering of saw-wrack the male crab endured the effects of exposure as the day warmed. A spring tide, with all the shore uncovered he would be out of water for a longer time. Occasionally bubbles burst from between his mouthparts, whilst the winkles he was sharing his shelter with emitted little sounds as they adjusted the plates that closed their shells. Through a gap between the draping seaweed he could see a stretch of sand that might be worth investigating for worms when the tide turned and he was no longer vulnerable. Suddenly he was aware of vigorous activity. The weed cloaking the rock was shaking!

A large otter nosing under the draping weed emerged with the female shore crab in her mouth. The concealed male saw the female crab dropped by the otter onto the sand where she defensively raised her pincers before scuttling sideways. Two smaller otters pounced on it, playing with it briefly before one bit into the brittle shell. The male crab shrank back amongst the concealing fronds. Unable to escape with the tide still out, he was totally vulnerable.

A bristly face inquisitively penetrated the weed. The shore crab raised its pincers in futile self-defence, but was pulled triumphantly from its hiding by a young otter. Just at that moment the sea lifted the bent straps of kelp, and advanced again towards the rocks. But the tide had turned too late for the shore crab.

The walk to Carsaig Arches

Described as 'the most beautiful coastal scenery in Britain' Mull has over 300 miles of coastline, mostly high cliffs and rocky platforms but also some notable sandy bays and coves. Visitors are able to walk many stretches of coast and one popular choice is to see Carsaig Arches at Malcolm's Point on Mull's southern shores.

There are two ways to reach the Arches and both involve long walks along narrow boulder-strewn paths. Strong boots, a map, a picnic, and a camera, are all recommended. The first and most popular route is to walk west from the pier at Carsaig, (GR 538217) heading towards the dark basalt sands of Carsaig Bay.

You may be tempted to linger and enjoy the delights of this beach but the towering cliffs act like a magnet and draw you on across beds of Jurassic shale exposed at low tide. Look down and you may see fossil ammonites, belemnites and bivalves – relics of when this part of Mull was once covered by a shallow tropical sea 200 million years ago. Leave them there for others to enjoy and follow the track onwards. Giant basalt columns in the ancient lava flows stepped above the grey shale and honey coloured sandstone, rise to heights that will make you dizzy when you look up at them.

For some they resemble descriptions from a fantasy novel. Dwarfed by forbidding cliffs you will be awed by Nature's raw magnificence.

The nine-mile walk (there and back) is largely at sea level and easy to follow along the narrow track made by the wild goats that live there. Apart from a scramble over one large rock fall, the walk is not difficult. At low tide part of the walk can be made over exposed Jurassic beds and at (GR 525204) the grey sandstone was quarried until 1873. Monks from Iona used the Nuns' Cave, (GR 524205) cut into sandstone cliffs by the sea at the end of the Ice Age and now high above sea level, as their workshop. Once they carved ornamental stonework to be seen today as tombstones, and carved facings at Iona Abbey and elsewhere. Goats use the cave as shelter today.

Headlands conceal your destination, but once you have skirted the last deceptive bluff you find yourself at what appears to be the end of the track. The first arch, a massive sea-breached promontory tantalisingly hides the second. You can view this arch from the high rock platform you walk across, but don't risk climbing down to explore or you may be caught by the Atlantic swell! Great care must be taken if you want to climb over the steep headland to see the second arch.

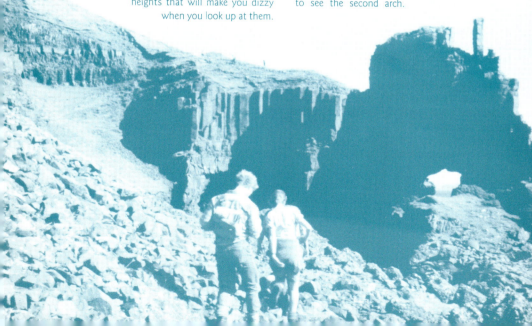

Many walkers arrive at this point, delight in the magnificence of their surroundings, discover smaller but intriguing wave-sculptured rocks, and happily return. Others, with time, and a head for heights, venture over the top and find the scramble worth the hazards. But be warned: it isn't advisable to attempt this in wet or windy conditions.

The second route, an approximate six-mile return journey, is shorter, but harder going and leads directly to the more unusual of the two arches. This walk takes you via the cliff top to the west of Malcolm's Point and its initial steep grassy route leaves you gasping in more ways than one. The views of the 900-foot high cliffs and the dazzling island studded sea are awe-inspiring.

To go this way you must turn off the Loch Scridain road at Traigh nam Beach and take the Forest Enterprise track through Glen Airigh na Searsain. Cars may be parked near the locked gate at the far end. For the first miles follow the track southwards over the Brolass plateau. A remnant of the highest lava flow, tilted landwards, caps the cliff, giving the loftiest point a slightly rakish appearance. Keeping this well to your left, follow a narrow sheep track towards ruined black houses at Airigh Mhic Cribhain (GR 477204). From here approach the cliff edge at its lowest point towards the south-west (GR 474196). You will see a burn, the Allt an Easa Criaracharain, disappear as a waterfall over the cliff top. Keeping a safe distance away from the dangerous cliff edge walk westwards to a very steep grassy gully, the only way down. Knees may protest, but the descent is rewarded by breathtaking views.

Once safely at sea-level, walk east towards a cove where the Eas Criarachain waterfall, leaping from the plateau, falls like a broken rhinestone necklace, dashing crystals of spray in your path. Backed by sheer cliffs the cove resembles a bite taken from the land by some prehistoric sea giant. Layer upon layer of horizontal lava flows are criss-crossed by two basalt sills creating a natural saltire – Mull's own 'cross of St Andrews'.

From here the route to the Arches is not long, but the first part is arduous. You have the choice of scrambling over stone runs on the green-skirted slope that rises steeply from the shoreline, or clambering through and over huge boulders on the beach. Unless you have one leg shorter than the other the beach route is actually easier! The route eventually levels off and a path leads around the rocky platform of Leac nam Leam (GR 491185) to the Arches.

When you round the headland and catch your first glimpse of the Arches, you'll wonder if you are seeing things. What on earth is a chimneystack doing perched on a sea arch? Is Nature having a joke? As you get nearer you can see that the 'chimney' is a column of basalt detached by the elements from the rest that form the arch top. The oddness of the massive arch is not entirely the result of its shape. The lofty crest thatched by tufts of sea-pinks, provides a safe haven for nesting sea birds, who look down with smug security. The doorway of the arch is shaped like a gigantic keyhole, and as you walk through, its enigmatic quality finally strikes you – waves only reach it at Spring tides. In common with all of Scotland, Mull's coastline is gradually emerging from the sea. Its companion arch, the headland of Malcolm's Point, is closer to sea level and more open to wave attack. You can walk through it at low tide.

Both routes to Carsaig Arches will provide you with vistas and experiences to enrich your memories.

Shipwrecks around Mull

Mull has a formidable rocky coastline, half of it facing the wild Atlantic. Submerged rocks and islets make these waters dangerous for the unwary in good weather, in bad weather they invite shipwreck. Most ships run for the shelter of the Sound of Mull but even here ships have come to grief. Including the famous Spanish galleon in Tobermory Bay, there are some 26 notable wrecks around Mull's coast, each with a tale to tell. A memorial to the men who sailed in them, these wrecks are not lifeless hulks but man-made reefs teeming with marine life, and divers from far and near enjoy the thrills and dangers of exploring them in Mull's clear waters.

1. **'Tobermory Treasure Ship'** – *a loss in every sense.*

The 'Tobermory Treasure ship' or San Juan de Sicilia was one of King Phillip II of Spain's Armada fleet of 1588 that fled around Scotland in the hope of getting home again. It ended its days when it was blown up in Tobermory Bay supposedly by a spy working for the English. The Macleans of Mull had given the ship safe anchorage for her to carry out repairs in return for the ship's mercenaries putting chief Lachlan MacLean's Clanranald enemies in the Small Isles to the sword. A few years later the Earl of Argyll, who had been living in Spain, returned home with information gleaned from survivors of the vessel and Armada manifests. He maintained the manifests listed war chests full of gold – including "30,000,000 of money". His claims sparked a treasure hunt lasting 400 years.

The history of treasure seeking

1608. The 7th Earl of Argyll, Admiral of the Western Isles, claimed rights of salvage. **1645.** The 8th Earl of Argyll, employed James Colquhoun, who successfully raised half a dozen iron guns.

1665. The 9th Earl of Argyll hired diving bell engineers James Mauld and John Sinclair who raised two brass cannons and a great iron gun. Further attempts under the 9th Earl between 1675 and 1683 resulted in anchors, cannons, bronze guns, the rudder, a silver bell, and the capstan being brought up – but real 'treasure' evaded them.

1686. King James II contracted divers Harrington, Penclarvis, Gelder and Souton, and they brought up 12 brass guns and other things "of no great value".

1688. William Sacheverell (later Governor of the Isle of Man) used a diving bell and brought up a gun, copper kettles, coins and plates.

1691-93. Goodwin Wharton attempted but failed to find anything.

1729-32. Jacob Rowe in his newly invented diving engine, (a large horn shaped copper tube with glass viewing window and holes for his arms in water-tight sheathing) was also unsuccessful.

1740. Jacob Rowe tried again in partnership with Archibald Grant and this time a 9'4" 23 pound French gun engraved with fleur de lys and 'Francis I of France' was brought up. (This is now at Inverary Castle).

1740-1814. More cannon and several iron balls were brought up, and Sir Walter Scott, visiting Tobermory, acquired part of the ship's timbers before the wreck finally disappeared beneath silt.

1871. The Marquis of Lorne (later the 9th Duke of Argyll) employed a diver by the name of Gush who retrieved some coins and a brass stanchion.

1873. A Norwegian barque 'brought up Spanish gold with anchor'. (Until this time any real treasure had eluded the hopeful seekers and methods of recovery had been primitive though damaging.)

What was to follow in the 20th century was thoroughly destructive.

1903-04. Captain Burns, representing a syndicate of Glasgow businessmen who hoped to become very rich on the gold they expected to find, used the steam lighter Sealight which used a sand pump to move the silt.

1905. Further exploration with the suction dredger Beamer brought up a swivel gun and many small items – but no gold.

1910-28. Lt. Col Kenneth Mackenzie Foss, another man obsessed by hopes of fortune established the 'Pieces of Eight' Syndicate, and also the 'Tobermory Galleon Salvage Company' luring investors with promise of plate, jewels, gold and silver. All the suction pump and mechanical grab on the Beamer brought up were iron shot, musket barrels, candlesticks, tongs and one gold ring. What Foss actually achieved with his wholesale methods was the final destruction of the San Juan yet the promise of unfound treasure persisted.

1954. A naval team under Commander Crabbe retrieved a few more artefacts, timber, lead sheeting, shot, an iron gun, pewter, and a skull.
1975-76. Commander John Grattan brought up pewter candlesticks, iron shot and lead sheathing.
1982 Wharton Williams Taylor of Aberdeen retrieved iron shot, bone, leather and shards.

The one piece of Spanish gold, an eight-reales of Phillip II that was recovered from the San Juan Bautista was presented to the British Museum its value far, far less than all the money spent searching for the fabled "30,000,000 of money". Sad to relate, this greed for the supposed 'Tobermory Treasure' has resulted in the destructive loss of the San Juan. Whatever is left of the Spanish ship can never be raised.

2. **HMS Dartmouth** – *Victim of stormy defiance.*
The warship Dartmouth, launched in 1655, was in service to King William and Queen Mary during the time of Jacobite sympathy in Scotland where it provided assistance to William's land based troops. In October 1690 the Dartmouth was sent to Mull to force MacLean of Duart to sign allegiance to William and Mary, but as it sailed into the Sound it encountered a violent storm and sought shelter in Scallastle Bay. For three days they rode at anchor but eventually the anchor parted and they were swept across the Sound to Eilean Rubha an Ridire where the ship smashed to pieces on the rocks. There were only six survivors from an estimated 130 on board. Discovered in 1973 the wreck was protected in 1974 and again in 1992. It has been explored archeologically by the University of St Andrews. Much of the wreck has been removed, including guns and the ship's bell for preservation but it still has much to be seen and is a favourite shallow dive for recreational divers.

3. **The Swan** – *A song still being sung.*
The Swan was a Cromwellian ship sent to teach Maclean of Duart and his clan a lesson. However, it capsized during a storm and sank in Duart bay. Privately discovered in 1979 but not made known until 1991 the wreck is the subject of detailed archeological exploration by St Andrew's University with help from the Dumfries and Galloway Diving Club. Finds from the Swan that include a 'Bellarmine' flagon, an ancient pocket watch, the intricately wired hilt of a sword, a pistol plate, carvings, and cannon balls can be seen at Duart Castle. It is hoped that a picture of naval life in Cromwell's days will be revealed as more historical artefacts from the Swan are brought up.

4. **The Mountaineer** – *Goes rock climbing!*

Mountaineer, launched in 1852, was a fast iron paddle steamer that worked out of Oban and served the west coast ports. In 1889, on her last run of the season she was making good speed and was within sight of Oban when, to everyone's amazement and distress she ran up and almost over the Lady Rock. Had she not run aground, but gone over, Mountaineer would have sunk immediately. Luckily there was no loss of life, all 40 passengers and crew being rescued. Much of her fittings and machinery were removed before she finally broke up in a storm.

5. **Grenadier** – *Caught off guard.*
The Grenadier, launched in 1885 was another popular paddle steamer. She served for many years taking day-trippers between Oban, Iona and Staffa. Grenadier 'consumed coal' and fire 'consumed' the Grenadier who sadly caught fire at her moorings whilst her crew were asleep at night in Oban harbour. The fire brigade could not quench the fire that spread rapidly, claiming the lives of three of the crew. She sank in shallow water at Oban's North Pier.

6. **Comet I** – *Rise and fall of a star.*

The Comet, which plied a regular passenger service through 'open waters', was one of the most famous ships in maritime history. Built on the Clyde and launched in 1812 it was a 25-foot wooden paddle-steamship, the first of its kind and as such an innovation when all other ships bore sails. She became very popular and was re-engined and lengthened to accommodate more passengers. In 1820, en-route between Glasgow and Fort William, at the end of the Crinan Canal, she was caught in a storm in the difficult waters of Dorus Mor. Her small engines were unable to cope with the atrocious tides and she was swept on to Craignish Point where she broke in two. Luckily all on board were in the section that remained aground and all managed to reach shore safely. Only the engine of Comet was eventually salvaged and presented to South Kensington Museum (now the Science Museum), where it can be seen prominently displayed today, in the 'Making of the Modern World' gallery.

7. **HMS Barcombe** – *A lucky rescue.*

On 13th January 1958 HMS Barcombe, having taken part in the rescue of HM Submarine Taciturn aground in Campbeltown, was en-route to Rosyth when she ran aground at Loch Buie in fog. There had been a navigation error and their distress call indicated that they were aground on Oronsay. Whilst rescue attempts centred first there and then around the Garvellochs, the 34 crew of HMS Barcombe endured 24 hours exposure to cold and rain, some on board the doomed ship and some on the rocky beach below a 300 foot cliff. It was only by chance that the fishing boat Rosebud on its way back to Oban from Tiree saw their flares and came to their rescue.

8. **The Minnie Knapp** – *An unsolved mystery.*
Suspicions of skulduggery surround the events that led to the loss of the wooden brig Minnie Knapp in June 1881. She sailed from Belfast insured for a sum far in excess of her value and loaded to the limit with 350 tons of limestone. Bound for the far north of Scotland she anchored in Tobermory before setting off, not for the Minch, but on a course through the treacherous channel between Rum and Canna. Unbelievably her captain continued tacking back and forth through the channel for 36 hours. Eventually she ran aground on Canna, was quickly re-floated and continued northwards, her crew pumping to control water leaking into the hull. Finally, they turned back to Ireland but in fine weather the captain put the exhausted crew on to a small boat whilst he, inexplicably, ran his ship ashore on Iona at the exact point where another Belfast ship had been lost. Was the captain incompetent or intent on wrecking the Minnie Knapp for the insurance money?

9. **The Ostende** – *Ross rocked by explosions.*
On the night of the 16th/17th of January 1943 the bow of Belgian ship Ostende was severely damaged by an explosion 9 miles west of Skerryvore Lighthouse. She managed to beach in Loch na Lathaich near Bunessan, her number 1 and 2 holds deep in water. Loaded with war supplies from New York, including 500 tons of bombs and artillery shells, salvage tugs were dispatched to offload and repair her. Work went well until the 20th of January when the drifter Lydia tied up beside her. During the night crewmen and villagers of Bunessan and the Ross of Mull were awakened by explosions. Somehow Ostende had caught fire and the shells ignited tearing the ship apart. Two of her 48 crewmen died, the Lydia was destroyed athough her crew were saved. Incredibly, some cargo survived the explosions but all that was left of Ostende was a mass of twisted metal and scattered plates.

10. **Aurania** – *A wreck to dive for.*
HMS Aurania, a liner built for Transatlantic trade but requisitioned by the government during WWI had just completed its seventh wartime transatlantic crossing as a troop carrier and was returning on the 4th of February 1918 to New York for more when she was torpedoed by a German U-boat off the north coast of Ireland. Eight men in the engine room died instantly but the rest of the crew managed to abandon ship. HMS Aurania beached on to the shore at Donegal. From here she was re-floated and towed towards the Clyde but in a twist of fate her tow broke and she drifted northwards finally breaking up on Caliach Point. The Aurania is an impressive wreck site for divers.

11. **Robert Limbrick** – *Victim of a savage storm.*
On the 5th of February 1957, hurricane force winds swept the northwest. Caught in the storm were two trawlers from Milford Haven, the Robert Limbrick and the Westcar. Huge seas battered the vessels but they maintained radio contact as they decided to change course for the protection of the Sound of Mull. Wind-driven spray made it impossible for them to see and at nightfall both skippers decided to give up their dangerous attempt and to ride out the storm until daylight. During the night the skipper of the Westcar heard the radio message 'Mayday! Mayday! Mayday! Robert Limbrick hard aground'. Driven ashore by mountainous seas, the Robert Limbrick was found the next day, smashed on Quinish Point. None of her crew of 12 survived. With wind speeds of 120mph she had fallen victim to the worst storm in living memory.

Sea tales, folklore and legends of Mull

Sea tales, folklore, and legends were handed down over the centuries by the seannachie: genealogists and storytellers of Scottish clans. The tales survived, repeated over and over again around firesides, until the magic of the spoken Gaelic was written for people to read. Nothing can ever replace the seannachie and the way that they told these tales of mermaids, fairies, and foul deeds. They are best recounted in the dark, by a glowing peat fire, with the wind moaning outside.

A Fairy Story from Mull – The fairies at Burg

Fairies lived on Mull – some say they still do. Not good fairies with pretty gossamer wings, but strange ugly little fairies that were always up to mischief. A place renowned as a fairy hill is Dun Burg, on the southwest coast of Ardmeanach. A long time ago, a woman called Inary lived at Burg keeping house for her husband. She was working late one stormy night making woollen cloth when she sighed saying "Oh that someone would come from land or sea, from far or near, to help me make this cloth". Had she not been tired she would never have been so misguided, for everyone then knew that fairies listened for just such requests. Immediately there was a knock at the door and a strange voice cried "Good housewife Inary, open the door to me, for as long as I have, you'll get." Inary opened the door and a woman dressed in green entered and sat down at the spinning wheel. Immediately there was another knock and another fairy entered to work, and then another and another, until the room was full of green-clad fairies noisily working and demanding to be fed. So Inary fed them, but the more she gave them the more they wanted, and she could not get rid of them. When eventually she'd baked the last of her flour and meal and the fairies were still there she fled the house, braving the gale, and ran to see a wise neighbour. Having admonished her for inviting such fairy help he then told her how to get rid of them. She returned home and stood outside shouting "Dun Burg is on fire! Dun Burg is on fire! Dun Burg is on fire!" Whereupon, all the fairies rushed out of Inary's house to see smoke rising from the cliffs by Dun Burg. "Oh my children! My children will burn!" they shouted and they ran back to their fairy hill. Inary ran inside and bolted the door tight. However hard she had to work, she never again voiced a request for help – for the fairies on Mull were more hindrance than help. And even today, on windy days, the fairy hill at Dun Burg looks as if it's on fire – when the waterfalls reverse and blow back up the cliffs like columns of grey smoke.

A Sea Tale from Mull – The fisherlad of Tobermory

There once was a Tobermory fisherlad who loved a pretty girl who did not love him. Heartbroken he left home to live and fish in a lonely cove. After a year and a day, he hauled in his net and found tangled in it a very strange fish indeed - a tiny, beautiful mermaid. She pleaded to be released offering gold and precious jewels from her father's kingdom under the sea, but the lad said that what he wanted in all the world was his true love. Promising him that her father could grant his request the mermaid took him under the sea to meet him. The sea king gratefully gave the fisherlad a gold ring and promised him that within a year and a day he would have his true love. So the lad went home. Returning from his boat a few days later he saw a pile of what he thought was seaweed at his door, but it wasn't seaweed it was a young woman dressed in rags. She was not pretty but neither was she plain. The lad intended to send her away but she told him she had run away from a cruel new stepmother and she had no home to go to. So he took pity and let her sleep in a corner of his tiny house. Each day he left without a word to go fishing and each day he returned to find she had a meal prepared for him and the house was swept clean. Not a word did he say to her until one day he decided that it was foolish for two souls to abide together without speaking, so he talked, and she replied, and he told her about the mermaid and the promise of the sea king. After a while he told her to eat with him at his table - and she did. Then she took to coming down to the shore to help him beach his boat of an evening and to spread his nets, and he was pleased to have help. She arranged wild flowers in the house and planted a wild rose at the door, she asked him to buy glass for the windows to keep out the cold and some whitewash for the walls. He grumbled a bit, but was glad to find his home more comfortable. Eventually a year and a day were up and the girl, knowing of the sea king's promise to provide the fisherlad with a wife said sadly that she must go back to her father's house. The fisherlad was suddenly alone and his heart told him that he missed the girl very much. So he went looking and eventually found her at her father's house. Placing the sea king's gold ring on her finger he asked her to marry him. That evening they walked down to the shore and there they saw the little mermaid sitting on a rock. "Did you get your own true love?" asked the mermaid smiling. "I did so!" said the fisherlad "And here she is!"

A Legend of Mull – How the Lady Rock got its name

Long, long ago, a chief of Clan Maclean had a wife of whom he had tired. She was a Campbell and the sister of the Earl of Argyll. In the seaway near Duart Castle is a rock that the high tide covers, and here the unfortunate woman was abandoned. Unknown to her husband she was rescued and taken back to her brother who then plotted revenge. It is said that Sir John Campbell surprised and slew his brother-in-law Lachlan Cattenach Maclean whilst in Edinburgh. Whatever the truth of the legend, the rock has been called the Lady Rock ever since.